# EX TERI ORS

*Inger McCabe Elliott*

CLARKSON POTTER/PUBLISHERS

NEW YORK

# CONTENTS

*Introduction* 7

*White* 15

*Yellow* 29

*Tan* 41

*Orange* 52

*Red* 66

# EX TERI ORS

TO LOVA AND DICK

*"Savage nations, uneducated people,
and children have a great predilection
for vivid colors."*

JOHANN WOLFGANG VON GOETHE

*"'I wanted to paint the houses in
vibrant colors,' he declared. 'A red
Fifth Avenue, a blue Madison. Park
Avenue: Yellow. Why not?'"*

FERNAND LÉGER

*"A fundamental truth: man needs color.
Color is the immediate, spontaneous
expression of life...."*

LE CORBUSIER

Published by Clarkson N. Potter, Inc., 201 East 50th Street, New
York, New York 10022. Member of the Crown Publishing Group.
CLARKSON N. POTTER, POTTER, and colophon are trademarks
of Clarkson N. Potter. Inc.

Random House, Inc. New York, Toronto, London, Sydney,
Auckland

Manufactured in Japan

Design by Howard Klein

Library of Congress Cataloging-in-Publication Data

Elliott, Inger McCabe.
   Exteriors / Inger McCabe Elliott.
   1. House painting. 2. Dwellings—United States. 3. Color.
I. Title.
TT320.E44  1993                              92-9144
729'.4—dc20                                  CIP

ISBN 0-517-57440-3

10  9  8  7  6  5  4  3  2  1
First Edition

*Pink  78*

*Brown  92*

*Blue  105*

*Gray  114*

*Green  128*

*Multi  142*

*Epilogue by Nate McBride  157     Take a House and Change Its Color  158     Notes  160     Bibliography  161*

*Acknowledgments  166     Index  167     Credits  168*

# INTRODUCTION

The peninsula village of Stonington, on the Connecticut shore, has a long history of seafaring and exploration. Its early houses were built in the eighteenth century, and then Federal, Greek Revival, pseudo-Gothic, and Victorian styles followed along. There are two main streets and nearly all the houses on these as well as on the side streets of Stonington are white, light gray, light tan, or light yellow. There is one small colonial house that is painted red, and another, a fisherman's house, that is painted a glorious yellow, stolen directly from a child's crayon box. ■ My house, a 1760 Colonial, stands behind two plane trees with its cornflower blue and its bright white trim and its tangerine door. Passersby stop and look at the color, ask where it came from—a stain? a paint? some "secret formula"? As for the blue, it is inviting even on the most bitter and hoary of winter nights. On hot summer days it beckons when it plays off against the white trim and the gray cobblestones and, to one side, a clump of birch trees with white bark and green leaves.

When I first came to Stonington, I lived in a vast wooden church. The previous owner had painted the exterior white with black trim—covering the muted decor and dark shingles of Victorian times. When it came my turn to paint the church, I kept the white but changed the trim from black to blue. I added three bands of blue around the tower. Blue, the color of a baby's eyes on a summer day. Blue, my favorite color.

At my design and textile firm, China Seas, I developed "French blue" as a theme color, used it in fabrics and wall coverings as well as sheets and blankets and even in paint. I used blue in porcelain dinnerware and enameled cookware. Our China Seas letterheads were blue, and so were the showroom aprons and even the Frisbees we gave out to customers.

My Stonington saltbox had been painted battleship gray with green trim. It looked uninviting and cold. The green leafy plane trees are bare in winter, and the wind whips from the sea, spraying salt onto the rocks and grass. I wanted something comforting and primary. Red, I felt, was too strong, because the house faces the sunset. Yellow gave neither form nor playfulness.

So I began painting wide swatches of different blues on the street side of the house. Neighbors and strangers would wander by, expressing their preferences—mostly they didn't want blue at all. "This is a white town," they would say. True, whitewashing was the earliest form of house painting in America, but early New Englanders experimented with many other indigenous materials. They mixed oyster shells and white lead paint with water—and sometimes they even crushed blueberries in milk and water to produce a "Colonial" blue-gray. Even in the eighteenth century, the making of paint was a lengthy and expensive process. Customers had to buy oil, pigments, and other ingredients separately and then hope that the combination would not congeal before the paint job had begun. The Stamp Act of 1765, which most people associate with the Boston Tea Party, also imposed a duty on imported paint. That spurred domestic paint production, and soon American paint makers were mixing a whole array of colors. Some of the most common colors were pearl, king's yellow, Indian red, and umber. For fancier tastes, there were Dutch pink, ultramarine, purple red, and indigo. A visit to Old Deerfield, Massachusetts, or to Benefit Street in Providence, Rhode Island, will confirm the colorful tastes of our ancestors.

Thus, when I chose "Persian blue" for my Stonington house, I was not exactly flying in the face of tradition.

From rosy-fingered dawn to wine-dark sea, poets have tried to capture color; with spectroscope and formula, scientists attempt to calibrate it. Isaac Newton tied the seven colors of the rainbow to the seven notes of the diatonic scale, claiming that the color red corresponds to the C note—which in turn corresponds to the planet Mars. The painter Wassily Kandinsky compared the colors with musical instruments; to him, yellow evoked the trumpet, red the cello, and blue the flute. Goethe thought he could almost taste color: blue would be like alkaline on his tongue. And Helen Keller once compared color to smell: "I understand how scarlet can differ from crimson because I know that the smell of an orange is not the smell of a grapefruit."

From Babylon to Byzantium, from ancient Greece to ancient Rome, from Egypt to China, generation after generation passed on the symbolism of color. White was purity, simplicity, and charity— except in Asia, where white became the color of death. Black was associated with mystery, terror, and doom. Blue meant mercy, hope, peace, serenity. Red was strength, earthy and life-giving. And green, which combined the blue of mercy and the yellow of beauty, represented triumph and fertility.

Colors are forever sending us signals. The stop sign is red with white letters because red quickly catches the eye. But when a dangerous curve lies around the corner, the sign is yellow with black lettering because yellow is the most visible of colors. On a sweltering day at the beach, we gravitate to the blue chair because it is "cooler" than either the red or the yellow one. Even insects have their color preferences. Flies will avoid horse stalls painted pale colors, especially blue. And mosquitoes bite those who wear dark blue and brown, but find orange, yellow, and white distasteful.

Since prehistoric times colors have been used to decorate everything from the human body to caves to public buildings. Almost any substance—vegetable, animal, or mineral—that can impart color was used. The cheapest and most accessible source was the earth itself, with its bountiful minerals— iron oxide, for example, probably the most common mineral in the world, produces English red. Other important mineral colors are sienna and ocher, both seen on the exteriors of houses from northern Norway to southern Sicily.

Umber, also extracted from the earth, can be brown (its natural state) or red (when burned) and can be used as a mixture to change the quality of other colors. Green earth was used in frescoes and the glazing of celadon.

Our ancestors found color in vegetation and animals as well. Dried insects yielded carmine red, and buckthorn berries produced turmeric and saffron. The charred wood of deciduous trees made a splendid and cheap black pigment, and charcoal from animal bones made bone black, which was applied to both the interior and the exterior of houses. White often came from chalk or white lead. The latter was poisonous, yet was applied to the faces of seventeenth-century Dutch prostitutes and Kabuki dancers of Japan as well as to homes. Most imaginative perhaps was Pliny's formula for the color red—to represent blood in painting. In his *Natural History* he suggested that an artist take the commingled blood from an elephant and a dragon that had slain each other in mortal combat!

Even without going to such extremes, making pigments was a long and laborious process—mixing water with a mineral, letting the concoction sit, skimming off the water, repeating the process five or six times, and finally grinding and drying the residue on a flat stone or glass. The resulting fine-grained powder resisted fading and became the basis for a variety of paints. Mixed with linseed, olive, or cod liver oil, it produced a form of oil paint; with egg, glue, and water, it became tempera; and with animal glues and water, it was watercolor.

Not surprisingly, people often picked colors for their houses according to what was close at hand. In the southwestern United States, for example, red clay hills and black loam valleys offered material and color with which to build adobe houses. In England, pink and red houses abound in the west and east, umber-colored houses are found in the north, and the south is rich with ocher hues. For the rich, colors varying from ivory to ultramarine—made from lapis lazuli—were available by the end of the eighteenth century. Prussian blue (also known as Paris blue and Berlin blue), chrome yellow, and that very beautiful but lethal color arsenic green were also on the market. Nearly one hundred years later, Prussian blue and chrome yellow were combined to make a lustrous and safe chrome green.

Color has always been used abundantly on buildings: any ancient building of importance and pretension was treated in the richest, brightest colors and these colors were applied in their full strength. Herodotus described the city of Ecbatana, built in the fourth century B.C. and layered in colors almost like a pousse-café: white at the bottom, then black, red, orange, gold, and silver at the pinnacle. Greek temples were painted in greens, blues,

reds, and yellows. The eighteenth-century discovery of Pompeii and Herculaneum proved that Rome, like Greece and other ancient civilizations, also used color on its buildings. Even Notre Dame cathedral, which now looms gray over the Ile de la Cité, was once covered, both inside and out, in brilliant colors. Thousands of miles to the east in the Middle Kingdom, the Chinese painted the imperial walls of the Forbidden City a vivid crimson, and tiled its roofs with bright yellow and blue.

With the Reformation in the fifteenth century, color began to disappear from European buildings, especially religious ones: reformers bent on expunging sensuous or pagan overtones found color too sexy and atheistic. Calvinists and Puritans joined in the battle against pigmentation, and for hundreds of years only the natural colors of building materials were allowed to show. Such religious fervor had another ally in Palladio, the sixteenth-century Italian architect, who thought that color was evil and that white was more acceptable to God; his splendid villas stand in haughty juxtaposition to the landscape. A century or so later, in England, Inigo Jones abandoned bright colors and fancy patterning in favor of "fair white."

All this whiteness was reinforced as Neoclassical architecture, with its stoas and pillars, became popular in the United States in the 1820s. But Counter-Reformation was not long in coming to the world of architecture. Suddenly a chorus of critics decried white as separating man from his environment or as signifying bad taste. In the view of critic and architect Calvert Vaux, Neoclassical white houses were evidence of a "vulgar desire for notoriety," and for John Ruskin, they symbolized "moral corruption and artistic decay."

So it was in the late nineteenth century that color came back into its own—but not just any color. Victorian tastemakers ruled that colors should come from the natural world, imitating soil, rocks, and the bark of trees: houses should show man living in harmony with nature. Formulas for the "proper" application of color were prepared by Victorians, spurred on by paint companies seeking markets for their ready-mixed products. With the advent of colored paint in cans that could be easily distributed to distant markets, the architect, designer, and paint maker, not the home owner, increasingly began to dictate how new houses should be painted.

Then came the Modernists, ushering in the twentieth century, discarding the ornamentation and color of the Victorians. More than anyone, perhaps, the Dutch painter Piet Mondrian influenced the concept of color and the form of architecture in the twentieth century. He introduced a new geometry of stark primary colors defined by a black-and-white grid. Designers followed suit, using red, blue, and yellow—as well as black and white—as a way of signifying spatial control. To the Bauhaus architects of the 1930s, both geometry and color were governing ideas. Architects such as Le Corbusier used brilliant colors in their work, while others, such as Mies van der Rohe, designed angular buildings with monochromatic tones.

Barely two decades later, white was back again. Why the rebirth of white? In part, because to many modern architects, builders, and even home owners, color had become the enemy of form; they thought it detracted from the shape of the house. Architect Hugh Hardy took critical note of this phenomenon: "Nature has enhanced this planet with such a profusion of color it seems strange that for thirty years architecture had so little of it," he wrote in the 1970s. Hardy helped lead the way back to color again as he and post-Modernists such as Luis Barragán, Robert Venturi, and Michael Graves came to view the surface of a house as a canvas on which to work their colorful ways.

To these architects—and to me—color is form's companion, enhancing shapes that otherwise might be lost. A sloping red roof defines the whiteness of a farmhouse on the coast of Oregon, for example, while creating a harmony with the natural surroundings. Just so, I think, does the blue of my house in Stonington effectively articulate its Colonial form.

The history of American architecture demonstrates the most important but elusive principle of good design. It must do more than simply harmonize color, form, and composition; it must astonish. Like a fine photograph or a painting, it should cause the viewer to stand back and say, "I never saw the world like that."

Not all designs, photographs, and paintings—and not all houses—are works of art. In this book I have tried to choose houses that please, surprise, and comfort the beholder as they nestle appropriately in their surroundings. A few of them are familiar as icons of good design, but most have not been discovered before. Their colors derive from natural materials—the orange of New Mexican adobe, the tan of Newport marble—and from paints and stains, from the imagination of the owner or architect.

# WHITE

White is the absence of color, yet it is probably America's favorite hue for houses. Its soaring popularity began in the Greek Revival era of about 1830 to 1855, when America embraced the notion of Neoclassicism that had swept Europe a few decades earlier. Mistakenly believing that the ancient Greeks had built pristine white temples—the Acropolis and other monuments were actually brightly polychromed—architects like McKim, Mead, and White created sparkling public buildings with marble columns; local builders from New England to Georgia to Ohio erected private homes with dentiled cornices, wooden porticos, and clapboard siding all painted white. ■ Whatever the building style on which it is applied, white is distinguished by its ability to reflect light: the glow of a sunset, the hue of an adjacent structure, the green of foliage. White can change mood, from playful to prim, from blaring to serene, depending on the type of house, its location, and even the color of its trim.

*On a spectacular promontory in Maine, the engineer-owner built a white lighthouse and pitched his house around it.*

PRECEDING PAGES: *Black windows and a dark gray roof cast a white wall into sharp relief on a building in Tyringham valley, Massachusetts.*

*In Miami Beach, Florida,* ABOVE, *kelly green trim gives a mundane white stucco building a jaunty personality.*

*Near Stockbridge, Massachusetts, architect Warren Schwartz built a monolithic white house for himself and his wife,* RIGHT. *The five-foot aluminum scuppers piercing the brow of the 1,200-square-foot octagonal tower act as practical but stylish waterspouts.*

In the inky shadows of a primeval Pacific Coast forest, a white house reflects the maximum amount of light, OPPOSITE. A sloping red roof accentuates the pallor of the walls and the soaring chimneys.

Igloos, ABOVE, are white-on-white—hard snow mortared together with loose snow. Primarily used as hunting lodges, they can be erected in just a few hours.

Green shutters and red mullioned windows distinguish many traditional white farmhouses in the northeastern United States, ABOVE RIGHT. The white barn next door, RIGHT, echoes the sharp lines of the house.

A tepee—a simple form once made of tanned buffalo hide and now made of canvas—stands out in white against the sky and dry scrub of Nevada County, California, LEFT.

Nautical-stripe awnings provide shade, as well as a bit of humor, on a white Colonial house on Long Island, ABOVE. In a burst of annual patriotism, the owners paint the shutters red one year and blue the next.

Modernist architect Richard Meier believes that white is the color that shows form to its greatest advantage. In the Malibu, California, house, RIGHT, the undulating lines and geometric forms of his design stand out against sky and grass.

*Red trim gives white doors in Key West, Florida, the appearance of columns,* LEFT.

*On a 100-acre horse farm on Johns Island, South Carolina, a Tuscan-looking tower,* ABOVE LEFT, *is made of all-American materials: white concrete blocks, plywood siding, and red asphalt shingles.*

*Before the hurricane blew its top off in 1938, the handsomely proportioned Connecticut tower,* ABOVE, *was one story taller.*

*On the veranda of a Georgian Revival– style house,* OPPOSITE, *variations in light transform uniform white paint into shades of honey, cream, ivory, and buttermilk.*

As in a Milton Avery painting, the aqua horizon and turquoise sea set off simple wooden shutters encased in a brilliant white stucco facade, ABOVE.

Rising from a hollow, three gangplanks thrust from architect Brian Murphy's white stucco house to a terraced hillside, RIGHT, in Santa Monica Canyon. Rigging, portholes, masts, and shrouds are appropriate words to describe this excitingly irrational building.

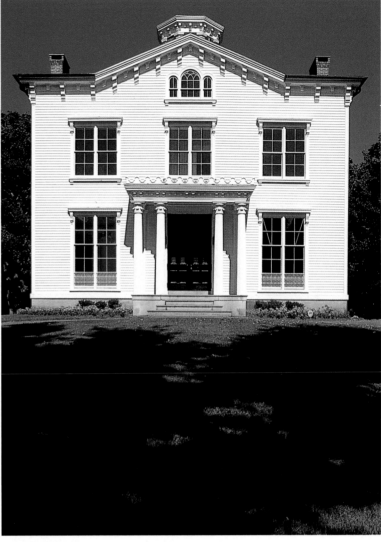

White Corinthian columns, illuminated by the September afternoon sun, form the dramatic portico of a Newport, Rhode Island, mansion, ABOVE. At sunset, the noble columns appear yellow at the edges; in the shade, they seem gray.

Greek Revival houses were originally painted white because home owners were under the misguided impression that ancient Greeks lived and worshipped in pristine white buildings. The circa 1830 Palmer House in Stonington, Connecticut, ABOVE, built by a sea captain, has been painted white for more than 150 years.

*The sun, which sees all things and hears all things.*  —HOMER

# YELLOW

One of the three primary colors, yellow is found everywhere in nature—predominantly in the rich minerals of the earth. Both inexpensive and durable, yellow ocher pigment has been used since ancient times to decorate the interiors of caves as well as the exteriors of temples. In imperial China, yellow was reserved for the emperor because he symbolized wisdom, enlightenment, and the power of the sun. In the United States, yellow is often seen on homes in Florida and California, where building styles have been influenced by Mediterranean antecedents. With terra-cotta barrel tiles completing the earth-tone palette, these American versions of Italian villas and Spanish haciendas are at once exotic and natural. ■ As a paint color, yellow provides versatility as well as risks. The neon-bright shade called chrome, once derived from lead, is at once cheerful and overpowering. Mustards are more sophisticated, but they can be bilious if not perfectly mixed.

*In Los Angeles, a yellow window is a friendly note in an unfriendly jumble of asphalt shingles and corrugated steel.*

PRECEDING PAGES: *A golden beacon with a Colorado mountain view was created by artist Pat Patterson.*

*The owners of a Maine farmhouse,* RIGHT, *painted both their home and their barn an appealing combination of yellow and white.*

*A twelve-over-twelve white window,* OPPOSITE, *in an eighteenth-century house in Providence, Rhode Island, accents cream-yellow clapboards.*

*The interior walls of a studio on San Juan Island, Washington, glow through a grid of glass and steel,* BELOW.

In Death Valley, California, a golden yellow house and its blood red trim mimic the intense desert heat. The smaller the building, the more intense the color appears, ABOVE.

Chrome yellow shutters cast a warm glow on white clapboard walls of the turn-of-the-century house, RIGHT. A yellow-and-white–striped awning completes the color scheme.

A yolk yellow door brightens a dreary winter day on New York City's Gramercy Park, ABOVE.

The green trim on a hearty lemon yellow house in Maine, RIGHT, *ties the building to the landscape, echoing the giant pine trees in the background and the emerald lawn in the foreground.*

A suburban Florida house designed by architect Steven Harris, ABOVE, lacks architectural detail, suggesting perhaps that a mustard yellow stucco wall gives as much presence to a house as applied decoration. Stucco was used by the Aztecs of Mexico, as well as by the Roman builders of Hadrian's Villa. The word is applied to any number of hard exterior finishes made of water mixed with cement, mortar, plaster, gypsum, lime, or fine sand and is a popular building material in warmer climates.

A clapboard facade painted butter yellow becomes an abstract painting with the help of an electric meter, RIGHT.

*Artist Robert Dash bought a sixteenth-century curved and flanged door for his home on eastern Long Island,* RIGHT. *Unlike the more subtle color he uses on his canvases, Dash painted the door a dazzling yellow—with black hardware—and then framed it with a lime green molding.*

Few architectural styles beat the stark simplicity of an eighteenth-century New England home. To emphasize its yellow color, the window trims, a beam, and two posts are painted white. The blue door adds to the charm and childlike quality of this old farmer's house.

Khaki yellow paint, RIGHT, calls attention to a doll-size house located in Saratoga, New York. The slender symmetry of the eaves and the checkerboard railing match the small scale of the building. The color of the awning is so close to the color of the walls that the awning is practically invisible.

The stridency of a mustard yellow porch in Stockbridge, Massachusetts, is muted by cooler accents: comfortable old furniture in black and gray, BELOW RIGHT.

*Things are seldom what they seem, / Skim milk masquerades as cream.* —W. S. GILBERT

# TAN

Cream, tan, taupe, beige—these "neutrals" are found in wood, stone, and earth. Often, the presence of tan signifies that materials have weathered or aged, taking on shades chosen for them by the elements. Cedar, teak, and mahogany, for example, are woods often used in shipbuilding because of their resistance to decay, even when exposed to moisture. Used untreated on the exteriors of houses, these tropical woods turn a soft, warm tan or silvery gray. Even stone shows the effects of the passage of time: pristine white marble may turn an elegiac shade of fawn in the course of a century. Stucco—a cementlike surface that is often painted—may be treated with pigment to resemble stone, or to blend with stone elements in the rest of the structure. ■ Collectively, the white-and-brown combinations that make up the neutral colors whisper rather than shout. Projecting a certain modest dignity, a tan house seems to proclaim what it is and to anticipate what it will become with age.

*In Miami, a Moorish influence can be seen in the red tiles, hint of a minaret, and thick cream stucco walls of a 1930s seaside villa.*

PRECEDING PAGES, LEFT: *Accidental aqua makes tan stucco worth a second look.*

PRECEDING PAGES, RIGHT: *The typical board-and-batten construction of a house in Dorr County, Wisconsin, designed by architect Thomas H. Beeby, is stained tan for the board and red for the batten— which covers the joint of two boards. This odd combination of colors gives both a vernacular and a vertical feeling to the house.*

*For clients in West Beth, Maine, Boston architect Andrea Lears designed a sleek tower capped with a smart red asphalt shingle roof,* ABOVE. *The tan walls are actually unweathered tongue-and-groove cedar siding, but they look surprisingly similar in tone and texture to stucco or stone.*

*In Encinitas, California, a pair of 1930s follies,* LEFT, *were designed to look like old fishing boats.*

*In another towering house,* OPPOSITE, *this one in Florida, architect George Hernandez used three stuccos—tan, cream, and white—giving each plane a presence that seems more structural than decorative.*

A magnificent Roman Doric portico, ABOVE, protects the entrance to a mansion designed for the Inman family of Atlanta, Georgia, by architect Philip Trammell Shutze in the 1920s. Inspired by eighteenth-century Palladian models, the facade is made of golden Italian limestone that changes color depending on the light.

Classic New England doorways, ABOVE, are simple and refined experiments in the Palladian mode. Cream paint makes the sensual carving and swirling pediment of this eighteenth-century example shine above the gray clapboard and rough-hewn stone steps.

Nearly sixty years after it was built in
1936, Frank Lloyd Wright's Fallingwater, ABOVE, remains a seminal house in
American architecture. It was erected over
an existing waterfall in the woods of Bear
Run, Pennsylvania, and is wrapped with
bands of tan concrete.

One of the bands, in close-up, RIGHT,
is actually a balcony that juts out over
the waterfall.

Modeled after the Petit Trianon at Versailles, Marble House in Newport, Rhode Island, LEFT, was built in the 1890s by Richard Morris Hunt as the summer residence for New York social leader Alva Erskine Vanderbilt. The name of Mrs. Vanderbilt's house is apt, for its walls are clad in more than 500,000 cubic feet of white Italian marble, now turned tan. As the day progresses, the marble walls turn from tan to a rosy beige, reminiscent of Jerusalem stone.

An early nineteenth-century house in New England, RIGHT, has finely carved wood pilasters applied to its brick facade. The wooden elements are not painted to blend with the brick, but are colored a contrasting shade of tan-gray to emphasize their lyrical form.

*In Deerfield, Massachusetts, a somber tan house built in 1740 sports a magnificent mocha-colored, hand-hewn door,* LEFT.

*A simple New England Colonial house,* ABOVE LEFT, *was stripped to reveal honey-colored wood and stained to ensure that the siding would not fade to gray.*

*The hallmark of Boston architect Henry Hobson Richardson's Romanesque buildings was his use of solid masonry construction, as in the gate house,* ABOVE.

*On Long Island, a house designed by Charles Moore in the 1960s,* OPPOSITE, *shows how sun and rain affect color: the old, raw wood walls have bleached to a dark gray and the new pine deck will change as soon as the wood weathers.*

*Orange is like a man, convinced of his own power.*   —WASSILY KANDINSKY

# ORANGE

The fruit that the Romans called the golden apple is both astringent and sweet, and the color named for the fruit likewise has strident as well as delicate moments. A blend of the primary colors red and yellow, orange can be hot, blatant, and bold, but, muted with white, orange becomes the calm, comfortable hue of peach. Peach is a popular color mostly used for interiors. On exteriors it can be startling. ■ Orange is intensified by light, and light more than location may determine how it is used. In the Southwest, where the warm tan hues of adobe often predominate against a backdrop of hills of the same coloration, walls or wooden details painted orange increase the sense of heat. In the Northeast or Midwest, a sunset might burnish the side of a white or cream-colored building, figuratively setting it afire with a wash of orange, enhanced by a flickering reflection in the windowpanes.

*The raw blond logs of an Alaskan cabin glow orange in the strong light of a setting sun.*

PRECEDING PAGES, LEFT: *At Putnam Cottage in Greenwich, Connecticut, eighteenth-century fishscale shingles are saturated with thick layers of earthy orange paint.*

PRECEDING PAGES, RIGHT: *Blood orange walls are heightened by dashes of black, olive, and glossy white in a French Quarter house in New Orleans. Although the wall is stucco, its color is bright and true because the color was painted on, not mixed in.*

*The drab tan siding of this building at Hancock Shaker Village in Massachusetts,* ABOVE, *conforms to the Shakers' rigid esthetic rules, but the evening sun turns the clapboard a vibrant orange.*

*In New York City,* OPPOSITE, *an urban dwelling is sheathed in orange metal panels. The geometric shadows of commercial light fixtures emphasize the unyielding industrial quality of the material.*

In Taos, New Mexico, yellow predominates in the orange of the adobe, ABOVE and RIGHT, offset by the silver of the beams.

In Santa Fe, assertive adobe walls, RIGHT, are of a different orange, nearly a burnt sienna. The heavy color makes the building seem as if it somehow was heaved from the earth, not built.

Andrew Batey, who with Mark Mack designed this home, OPPOSITE, *studied with the great Mexican architect Luis Barragán, whose influence may be seen in the exterior staircase and blocks of color.*

*Even without the provocative billboard, the split-level orange and red of a city building,* ABOVE, *suggests its gentrification.*

*White window frames absorb much of the chromatic thunder of an orange wall,* ABOVE RIGHT, *making the orange appear duller than it really is.*

*Full-length orange shutters, painted on both sides, dress up the sober buff facade of a French Colonial building in New Orleans,* RIGHT. *Even the orange graffiti seems part of the scheme. Fine green ironwork is customary in New Orleans Greek Revival architecture.*

A mandarin orange house near Catfish
Row in Charleston, South Carolina, LEFT,
is complemented by gray-green shutters
and white trim. Whether the owner knows
it or not, the color trio is that found on an
orange tree—orange fruit, green leaves,
and snow white blossoms.

Smith/Thompson, Architects, accentuated the
asymmetrical brick front of an apartment
building on Seventh Avenue in New York
City, ABOVE, by painting it a rich sienna.

Near Albuquerque, New Mexico, in the Rio
Grande Valley, a home designed by Antoine
Predock in the southwestern vernacular
wraps an inner courtyard, the foundations
of its blushing walls lapped by a sea of
blue concrete, RIGHT. The enclosed space
provides warmth in winter while mimicking
the parallel grids of the valley's agricultural
fields below. The "adobe" trellis is actually
stucco and wood.

An exuberant white frosting of baroque
scrolls and seashells decorates the salmon
walls of the Villa Constantia in Montecito,
California, a lavish Dutch Colonial–style
house built in 1930, ABOVE. The house also
gets a natural splash of orange from the
trumpet flower vine that clambers up its walls.

A *dreary tenement*, ABOVE, *is sparked by
deep salmon paint and blinding white
shutters. The functional but unappealing
fire escape disappears when painted to
match the surrounding walls.*

On the screen door of an eighteenth-century New England house, the eloquent geometry of an old iron latch is enhanced when set against a self-effacing background of soft peach, ABOVE.

Sturdy rose-colored walls of a small ski chalet near Lake Tahoe, Nevada, ABOVE, take on a playful air when joined by bands of yellow and chocolate—and a neon blue chair. The steep roof is common in snow country.

*And let's be red with mirth.* —WILLIAM SHAKESPEARE

# RED

Passion and power, blood and ardor, fire and war are but a few of the associations with the color red. To a Hindu, red means life and joy; to a Chinese bride, a red wedding dress brings happiness and good luck. Many nations have used red as an emblem of patriotic pride—in flags, helmet plumes, and soldiers' uniforms. A touch of rouge enlivens an ashen face. And red is the color of love, in the hearts and roses of Valentine's Day. Used outdoors, red has the virtue of being a primary color—a color of nature—but one that does not predominate in the landscapes of temperate climates. When the palette of summer is an array of greens, red—green's complementary color—contrasts strongly, heightening the forms of buildings against the backdrop of trees and fields. In the fall, red picks out the colors of changing foliage; in the winter, it is warm against the white snow. For making an emphatic statement, no color compares with red. Red tells us to stop, to look, and to listen.

*Warm red walls on an old Vermont farmhouse near Lake Champlain offer solace from the snow.*

PRECEDING PAGES, LEFT: *The bright color and unusual oval shape attract attention to a gate in Key West, Florida, a town better known for its pastels.*

PRECEDING PAGES, RIGHT: *The Nathan Hale schoolhouse in East Haddam, Connecticut, is a perfect example of how color looks different on different surfaces. On wood, red paint is scratchy and lined; on metal, it is smooth and dappled.*

*Red and gold, symbols of power, give a regal importance to a Victorian row house,* OPPOSITE.

*At what was once home to nineteenth-century sculptor Augustus Saint-Gaudens in Cornish, New Hampshire,* RIGHT, *the Greek-style balustrade and columns on the porch are snow white, but the floor is a startling Pompeiian red.*

*The red stucco walls of the historic Rosalie house in Eureka Springs, Arkansas,* BELOW, *provide a quiet backdrop for a magical confusion of cream, brown, yellow, and white gingerbread fretwork.*

*Few houses have roofs and walls of the same color. At a home in Lycoming County, Pennsylvania,* RIGHT, *red unites disparate building materials and calms a plethora of architectural elements.*

*Hanging ferns, cast-iron balconies, elongated windows, evergreen shutters, and ceiling fans identify the location of a painted red-brick building as New Orleans,* BELOW RIGHT.

*Climbing vines such as Virginia creeper soften the lines of buildings, require little maintenance, and in the autumn add spectacular color,* ABOVE.

*The dull brick of a New York City building is rendered less common by the odd white halos around each red-framed window, created when old windows were replaced with new,* RIGHT.

PRECEDING PAGES, LEFT: *A simple house and barn in Vermont are separated from the landscape by an outline of white trim.*

PRECEDING PAGES, RIGHT: *A mundane exterior becomes exotic when a layer of white snow settles atop red fire escapes for a striking two-tone effect.*

*Multiple reds achieve a stunning effect,* ABOVE.

*Textile designer Jack Lenor Larsen "grew" brilliant red wooden posts in his garden on Long Island,* RIGHT.

Blue-black wrought iron scorpions its way across a blood red door in New York City, ABOVE, *a fearless use of colors that are both passionate and scary.*

The dramatic door with its symbolic top, ABOVE, *was designed by husband-and-wife architects Tod Williams and Billie Tsien for a house on Long Island. The vibrant burgundy door glimmers like a warm campfire in a canyon of chilly grays, leading the visitor down the path, to the entrance, and into the house.*

*The very pink of perfection.* —OLIVER GOLDSMITH

# PINK

From Hollywood to Miami Beach, pink houses share a sense of fun, whimsy, and tropical ease. A pastel created by combining various shades of red with varying amounts of white, pink can take on a drama outdoors that it does not have indoors. Despite the outlandish or saccharine associations of pink, it has been used on house exteriors from Maine to San Francisco, from Idaho to New Orleans. As if to imbue the very meaning of "house" with an upbeat and even offbeat sense of humor, Americans have painted every conceivable house type—Colonial, Gothic, Spanish, and Victorian—with pleasing, friendly shades of pink. ∎ In fact, it is difficult to coax pink into behaving seriously. Paired with aqua and lilac or intensified with notes of black and white, pink defies rather than blends with most natural surroundings. Suggesting playfulness whether set at a resort or at an elegant mansion, pink almost always brings an element of surprise.

*A loft building in New York City resembles a flock of tropical birds when its pink shutters are flung open.*

PRECEDING PAGES: *A pink house rises from the planned community of Seaside, Florida.*

*In a Miami house designed by Arquitectonica,* RIGHT *and* BELOW, *pink takes on a bold personality against the blues of water and sky.*

*And not far away, the Art Deco–style Coronet apartment block has the hue of cotton candy,* OPPOSITE.

*So unrelieved is the chalky pink of this turn-of-the-century factory building in Newton, Massachusetts,* OPPOSITE, *that even the gray roof seems to take on a rosy glow.*

*In Taos, New Mexico, a gray grille and window punctuate a pink pressed-tin facade masquerading as cut limestone,* RIGHT, *an unusual use of a material normally found on indoor ceilings, not on the exteriors of houses.*

BELOW, *a bubble-gum–colored fence, balanced by aquamarine steps and shutters, lends a cartoon quality to an otherwise sober Colonial saltbox house in Rhode Island.*

The eccentric Gothic Revival rooflines, step gables, and ornate fretwork of the nineteenth century were meant to project a serious moral tone, ABOVE and RIGHT. This Victorian-era house "Rose Cottage" in Woodstock, Connecticut, contrasts chocolate brown doors and rose-colored trim, their symmetry broken only by an elegant china doorknob and matching keyhole.

In Santa Monica, California, OPPOSITE, architect Brian Murphy renovated an old seaside house in the classic Mediterranean style that works so well in the bright light and balmy air of the West Coast—candy pink walls, black wrought iron, and a jungle of pink and red geraniums.

*Lilacs create a subtle juxtaposition of pastels against a pink Taos wall,* OPPOSITE.

*Decades of rain and snow have washed white paint from the stone trim onto a Victorian brick facade, muting its red to pink,* ABOVE.

*For an Arizona client, architect Antoine Predock set a house into the earth, making the structure seem a natural outgrowth of its desert environment. The mauve volcanic stone pyramid,* ABOVE RIGHT, *reflects the subtle, shifting palette of this natural world.*

*Raspberry clapboard, strengthened by notes of black and white, creates an aura of frivolity in a prim Victorian house at Newburyport, Massachusetts,* RIGHT.

Powdery shades of pink and orange-red
give a hefty Santa Monica hacienda the
ephemeral quality of a mirage, LEFT, from
the weathered red of the curved terra-cotta
roof tiles to the ashes-of-roses shade that
tints the mottled stucco walls. Gray-green
trim ties this dreamlike house to reality.

Unattractive artifacts of the machine age,
ABOVE, almost disappear when concealed
with layers of raspberry paint.

Here is the side-view of an elegant
Tuscan-style mansion in Raleigh, North
Carolina, RIGHT. Windows arch, double-
decker porches line each side, and moss
green eaves cap a stylish house. Now
converted into governmental offices, the
house exemplifies an Italianate style
of architecture popularized in the mid-
nineteenth century by England's Prince
Albert, a noted Victorian connoisseur of
art and architecture.

# BROWN

Row upon row of stately single-family houses with elegant stoops are a notable part of the American urban landscape. Houses made of brownstone—in fact a reddish brown sandstone—lend the streets a somber dignity, according to architecture critic Vincent Scully. The extraordinary popularity of brownstone for Victorian town houses was partly due to its ability to hold its color under the onslaught of dirt and soot. More than one hundred years after its introduction in American architecture, most brownstone still retains its dignity. ■ In addition to stone, brown is seen in exteriors made of adobe brick—sun-baked mud and straw—and in paint derived from raw and burnt umbers. A mix of many colors, brown seems to work best in juxtaposition with red, blue, green, and white, which cheer its "somber dignity," or as a warmed-up shade of cinnamon against a cooler shade of gray. When sparked with unusual color, brown loses some of its sobriety and gains panache.

*A classic Dutch Colonial stone house in the Delaware River Valley takes its fertile colors from the surrounding countryside.*

PRECEDING PAGES, LEFT: *Water can often drastically alter the perception of color. Here the shimmering surface of a pond toys with the brown shade and texture of a farm building.*

PRECEDING PAGES, RIGHT: *Corrugated metal usually comes in shades of gray or silver, but a striking cinnamon brown variety wraps a dormitory for oil rig workers in Kenai, Alaska.*

*One can almost feel the warm, gritty surface of this deep brown adobe wall,* OPPOSITE. *Its solidity is heightened by the complement of aqua windows and pale, sage-colored bushes.*

*In an unusual color combination, a matte battleship gray window frame and stark white muntins are set into a wall clad in unfinished brown clapboard,* ABOVE.

*A brown saltbox house in Millbrook, New York,* LEFT, *is somber and tidy, except for the wink of the window screen.*

Architect Charles S. Greene and his brother Henry M. Greene, leaders of the California Arts and Crafts movement (1905–20), designed the Gamble House in Pasadena, LEFT, with a concern for natural materials and fine craftsmanship.

The brown-painted window frame of a nineteenth-century house evokes the musty smell of an old book, ABOVE LEFT.

The unpretentious honesty of a natural wood door lightens a southern Greek Revival mansion in the garden district of New Orleans, ABOVE.

On a rambling 100-year-old seaside cottage built by local craftsmen in Hancock Point, Maine, shingles were stained to a rich sienna, OPPOSITE.

In South Carolina, thick white mortar between leather brown bricks gives an exterior a bold character, LEFT.

The tower of a New England gate house, ABOVE, appears brown because of the impressionistic melding of naturally weathered colors—green, tan, gray, puce, and burgundy.

Brownstone—red-brown sandstone—row houses are a beloved symbol of New York City's past because of their color as well as their human scale, OPPOSITE. Architecture critic Vincent Scully calls them "the very blood and fiber" of the city.

The strength of the farmhouse, OPPOSITE, lies not so much in its no-frills geometry as in the deep earth brown of its clapboards. The horizontal brown is strengthened by vertical gray silo rectangles.

Though modest and uncomplicated, a ghost ranch is hauntingly beautiful against the azure Colorado sky, LEFT.

On a house in Rhode Island is an intriguing and highly unusual color combination, and it works: bright cinnamon shutters, a steel gray clapboard, and white windows, BELOW LEFT.

A typical Virginia cabin, BELOW, becomes something special when the mud between the thin wooden logs is painted sparkling white.

*Blue color is everlastingly appointed by the Deity to be a source of delight.*   —JOHN RUSKIN

# BLUE

Blue, with yellow and red, is the third primary color. Originally derived from scarce vegetable and mineral pigments including lapis lazuli, few exteriors were painted blue becuase of the cost. Even now, Americans are cautious about using certain shades—violets and purples still project a regal air and are often reserved for popes and kings. ■ In places where sunny days are more frequent than rainy ones, the blue of the sky—which of course can vary dramatically in hue from place to place, day to day, and hour to hour—dominates the color scheme. Like fair skies, blues evoke peace and constancy. The blue house may appear to soar heavenward, suggest the refreshing coolness of a mountain lake, or, in its most vivid incarnations, offer a manmade contrast to nature's purity.

*A coat of glossy royal blue laid over a rougher layer of paint gives the frame of a simple screen door a mottled watery texture.*

PRECEDING PAGES: *The blue-and-white porch of a Pennsylvania farmhouse has the old-fashioned appeal of mattress ticking and striped awnings. Most exteriors are considered from the point of view of a passerby; here the stripes have the most striking effect from inside looking out, leading the eye from the interior to the threshold of nature.*

*On a sturdy early American house in Maine, OPPOSITE, soft and faded shades of blue— one for the shutters, another for the facade— bring to mind a hydrangea bush.*

*In Houston's sultry Texas heat, ABOVE, a blue-painted stucco house designed by architect Carlos Jimenez is a cool oasis. White windows and a white door help break up the solid blue structure, as do triangles of light tan.*

*Designed by the owners of Arquitectonica for themselves, this Miami house, RIGHT, is a field of bright geometric white stucco punctuated by blue details.*

Used to block a disintegrating gable, a functional patch of blue tin, ABOVE, brings a jewellike splash of color to the roof of an old barn near Roxboro, North Carolina.

Blue brick contrasts dramatically with the familiar red, white, and black of a bright urban landscape, RIGHT.

An unusual color for aluminum siding, royal blue takes on strikingly different hues in sun and shade in an otherwise plain suburban house, ABOVE and RIGHT.

A jangling combination of lavender, lime, and purple makes an abstract canvas out of a prosaic New York City exterior, LEFT.

Beyond a window set into a dusty purple clapboard wall are parrot green shutters, BELOW.

Like a chorus of angels, OPPOSITE, three stair windows capped by white and gray halos pierce the walls of a violet-blue home in Raleigh, North Carolina.

*Dear friend, all theory is gray.* —Johann Wolfgang von Goethe

# GRAY

To make his colors more luminous and to introduce contrast without muddying his canvases with black and brown, the great British landscape painter J. M. W. Turner relied heavily on grays and other subtle hues. Gray houses also make use of the illusion of light, sometimes appearing to glow as if illuminated from within. Many building materials—wood, stucco, stone, and tile—are gray, or become gray, without additional help from the painter's brush. Each shade of gray is slightly different, with particles of many other colors, and its hue can be manipulated: placed next to another color, gray will assume a tinge of its companion. Gray beside green will turn rosy; beside orange, blue. ■ Manmade grays, such as those in aluminum, steel, and metallic paints, may not convey this eerie luminescence. But even within a monochromatic color scheme, they provide a drama of their own, especially juxtaposed against natural elements, such as gray cement against weathered wood.

*A storybook white picket fence plays up the hard industrial texture of the exterior.*

PRECEDING PAGES: *From Hawaii to Maine, mobile homes are an integral part of America's landscape. They are perhaps the contemporary version of log cabins, which also reflected an economic and immediate need for shelter without regard to aesthetics. Here a reflective strip of corrugated aluminum blazes across the gray-green facade of just such a house.*

ABOVE: *On the facade of an Arizona house, towering expanses of gray cinderblock and stucco bring monumentality down to earth. Subtle chromatic desert colors—mouse, gray, mole—lessen the size of the house.*

*In a detail of a Santa Monica house,* OPPOSITE, *wood, metal, and a painted fence combine to take a commonplace building into the abstract, relating it more closely to modern art than to suburban architecture.*

Designed in 1914 by F. Burrall Hoffman, Jr., the Miami, Florida, mansion called Vizcaya, LEFT, is a vast Italian Renaissance villa, adapted to its subtropical setting with yellow-and-blue–striped awnings.

Connecticut architect John D. McVitty painted the shutters and facade of his house, ABOVE LEFT, the same shade of gray, knowing that they would appear to be different colors.

Streaks of soot on a somber gray limestone apartment building on Fifth Avenue, New York City, make it seem as venerable as the medieval palazzi of Italy, ABOVE.

Architect Ruben Ojeda's house in Mount Washington, California, OPPOSITE, is a citadel of gray-blue stucco.

PRECEDING PAGES, LEFT: *On the Willamette River in Portland, Oregon, a gray corrugated metal houseboat looks like an intergalactic spaceship.*

PRECEDING PAGES, RIGHT: *Architect Steven Holl surrounded a Minimalist house of weathered cedar on Martha's Vineyard with the skeletal elegance of a Chinese Chippendale balustrade.*

*Originally a stable, then a post office, this eighteenth-century Connecticut guest house,* ABOVE, *has not been painted for decades. Old gray paint on weathered wood gives a depth and presence that no modern techniques can equal, allowing this little house to blend in gently with the forest behind.*

Architect Frank Gehry created a space-age Stonehenge in Brentwood, California, ABOVE, *made up of room-size pavilions around a reflecting pool, some sheathed in white stucco, others in a silvery lead-coated copper, which will slowly oxidize to green. The proportion of the 5,700-square-foot house may seem unsettling, but the copper panels cause its mass to vaporize against the cloudy sky.*

Trowel marks in a gray-tinted stucco wall, ABOVE, *contribute to the intentionally unfinished look of an Atlanta house by Scogin Elam Bray Architects. The spectacular steel stairway painted with rust brown primer, the natural redwood window frames, and the lush grove of trees more than compensate for any potential blandness.*

A mauve Gothic Revival barn in Woodstock, Connecticut, LEFT, is decorated with brown gingerbread and a matching birdhouse perched on top.

When taken to its pallid extreme, gray can make a building seem a mere mist on the horizon. The hues of this blue-gray and white stucco residence on Long Island, ABOVE, by Tod Williams and Billie Tsien help it blend into the landscape of sky and nearby pond and bay.

The summer sun turns the shingles of a cottage in Sagaponack, Long Island, ABOVE, *from a light natural tan to a faint, luminous gray.*

*A gray door, its hardware and trim painted so as to disappear from view,* RIGHT, *forms a perfect rectangle in a wall so red it makes the gray seem almost blue.*

*My salad days,/When I was green in judgment.*   —WILLIAM SHAKESPEARE

# GREEN

On a visit to America in 1842, Charles Dickens expressed his amazement at finding the shutters of all white houses painted "the greenest of green." To this day, owners of white houses in rural New England still show a preference for green shutters, but few people paint their entire houses green. Even when advances in chemistry in the late nineteenth century made green paint more affordable than it was in Dickens's day, the color did not increase in popularity. Since the colors of nature always challenge a house, green houses tend to disappear into a green landscape, but this does not entirely explain why green has remained in disfavor. ■ Nevertheless, there are settings in which this lively mixture of blue and yellow, cool and warm, actually thrives, particularly in the tropics, where the warm light enriches aquas and limes so that they balance pinks and other pastels.

*Jade green paint transforms classic red brick.*

PRECEDING PAGES, LEFT: *A bright green doorway pops out of a sea of ultramarine blue on a Maine house.*

PRECEDING PAGES, RIGHT: *In Taos, New Mexico, another brilliant green door sits in orange adobe walls. Note how the green of both doors appears different because of dissimilar surrounding colors.*

*Green and yellow enliven the exterior moldings of a weathered shingle house,* LEFT.

*A totally green house in Houston, Texas,* BELOW, *is lightened by a scarlet door, scarlet railings, and—appropriately—a pair of ready-to-decorate Christmas trees.*

*In Marietta, Georgia, a green house shines in the night,* OPPOSITE; *an orange lampshade glows in the window—ample proof that what goes on inside a house affects the outside color as well.*

A Louisiana house keeps its secrets behind three green full-length wooden shutters, ABOVE, *each outlined in white and afloat on a sea of pumpkin-painted brick—an exciting and memorable combination.*

*The chalky moss green of a clapboard Providence, Rhode Island, house,* RIGHT, *is a near match for the tidy green bushes along its foundation. Crisp white window frames keep the facade from blending into the plants.*

*Stark brick walls can be hidden with
vegetation. In New York City, a lush
curtain of vines turns an apartment
building into a bush with windows,* ABOVE.
*In addition to color and texture, the ivy
gives the viewer—and the building—an
unending spectacle of movement, as wind
and rain rustle the leaves.*

The sea foam green walls of a New England
house, OPPOSITE, *keep the promise of spring
alive, even in the chilly depths of winter.*

In Northampton, Massachusetts, an
unwieldy relic of Victorian architecture,
ABOVE, *becomes almost graceful when
painted a delicate shade of almond green.*

On a farm in North Carolina, decades of
sun and rain have transformed the stained
surface of a rustic door into a shimmering
field of emerald greens and peacock blues,
RIGHT. *Rarely will any color stay true after
years of abuse from the elements, but often
the altered results are more appealing than
the original.*

Few homes are painted green because the color vies, usually unsuccessfully, with the incomparable greens of nature. A vivid green Waterford, Connecticut, house, touched with turquoise, ABOVE, looks best in winter snow.

Despite the long-standing bias against green exteriors, sea foam green is a popular color for homes in the northern and southern United States: it hints of tropical climes. On the coast of Rhode Island, a sea foam green house, ABOVE, is elegantly paired with cream.

A proper New York City brownstone became a flirtatious belle, ABOVE, *the moment its new owners painted the exterior a delightful shade of pale aqua.*

A small, green, temple-shaped house in Raleigh, North Carolina, RIGHT, *is an uncommon—and highly successful— departure from the white-temple norm.*

*In southern climates, amid glass and tile, green and aqua easily blend in a cool and shiny surface.*

*Light changes the color of everything, especially glass. At a Los Angeles house by Elyse Grinstein and Jeffrey Daniels, RIGHT, illuminated "aqua" glass treads form a stairway to a net-covered patio.*

*When applying a bold color, confidence is everything. A bravura splash of aqua on an otherwise ordinary New England shack gives it much needed animation and makes it memorable, OPPOSITE.*

*He best can paint them who shall feel them most.* —ALEXANDER POPE

# MULTI

Just as the ancient Greeks and Romans thought little of splashing their buildings—and

even their statues—with a rainbow of colors, some modern-day architects and just plain

home owners throw caution to the winds. These daring types look upon form and color as

inseparable and are not afraid to embellish one with the other, in sometimes startling ways.

They juxtapose colors to express mood and point of view, exploiting the power of oppo-

sites—blue and orange, purple and green. Sometimes they pair colors that are adjacent to

each other, such as yellow and orange, blue and green, to create a comfortable mood. While

a trio of primary colors may suggest childhood, a quintet of azure, magenta, golden yellow,

cream, and bittersweet orange implies a more complex and sophisticated scheme. Whatever

the final effect, each multicolored treatment demands the fine eye of an artist and the

daring of an aerial acrobat. Risk is an essential element.

*Craig Hodgetts and Ming Fung designed a house high in the Hollywood Hills with cubes in six explosive colors.*

PRECEDING PAGES: *Luminous steel on a house designed for artists by Harry Teague reflects a brilliant Colorado sky.*

*Architect Henry Killam Murphy modeled the house,* BELOW *and* RIGHT, *complete with filigreed doorway, after Beijing houses built during the Ming dynasty. The strong colors hold up admirably against the bright Florida sun— from brilliant Ming yellow roof tiles to scarlet columns and white stucco walls.*

*Painted with uninhibited colors—over the doors, around the windows, along the roofs—artist Mick Hagerty's plain bungalow takes on a swaggering, childlike bravado. This is an excellent example of how a sensitive colorist makes use of an everyday object—in this case, a cabin— as a personal canvas,* OPPOSITE.

In Paoli, Pennsylvania, near Valley
Forge, a concrete tower stands alongside
a simple dark brown wooden house, LEFT.
As planned by the late owner, Wharton
Esherick, the tower's dappled camouflage
paint job neatly reduces its oppressive bulk
while just as neatly making reference to
the surrounding multicolored foliage.

Tropical climates call for an engaging array of tropical hues. ABOVE, a silvery aluminum, blue, pink, and aqua structure perches atop wooden floor beams, their ends carved in the shape of porpoises.

Prefabricated and easily accessible modules were first assembled by Ray and Charles Eames in 1949 when they designed and built what was destined to become a classic American home, the Stock Part House. Composed of transparent, translucent, primary-colored glass and stucco panels, the Eames home in Pacific Palisades, California, RIGHT, could have come from a canvas by Piet Mondrian.

*In the northeastern United States, traditional shades of turquoise, red, and cream,* ABOVE, *combine for an unusually lusty effect—far from what the colonial forefathers intended for their architecture.*

*A tiny cottage in a summer colony on Martha's Vineyard distinguishes itself from its neighbors with salmon-colored gingerbread, a slate blue porch floor, and pale blue chairs,* ABOVE .

*Rust and rustication: painted sheet
metal lives harmoniously in the southern
United States,* ABOVE.

In the boulder-strewn desert of Joshua Tree National Monument in California, designer Josh Schweitzer and colleagues designed a feat of abstract architecture, LEFT *and* BELOW LEFT. *Colors were chosen for each pavilion for their specific meanings: orange from the desert sunsets for the patio, olive green from lichen for the living rooms, and royal blue from the sky for the sleeping rooms.*

*More than ten shades of blue, brown, yellow, green, and gray combine in the tiled wall at Fonthill, the house-cum-museum of Henry Chapman Mercer in Doylestown, Pennsylvania,* OPPOSITE. *Even the letters above the lintel are multicolored, and the peeling, faded door has five shades of blue.*

FOLLOWING PAGES, LEFT: *In a Maine gate house, a rich blue wooden doorway with a matching clerestory window is framed by large gray stones, with bands of red stone making a radiant pattern not unlike a sunburst. Colors and textures combine to form a successful whole.*

FOLLOWING PAGES, RIGHT: *Built in 1725 in Springfield, Massachusetts, and moved in the 1950s to nearby Deerfield, the historic Dwight House is built of wood and has a slate gambrel roof. Its basic palette is the gray of the roof and the cream of the clapboard. Window and door trims are gray, but the window muntins and sashes, as well as the doors, are bright red-orange. To ensure that no one misses the point, a red line has been painted under the eaves and along the sides of the house. This is a truly imaginative and fearless facade.*

# EPILOGUE

The exteriors of our homes, like the clothes we wear, are reflections of ourselves.

A periwinkle saltbox in a white New England village, a wave of gray corrugated metal in a sea of bungalows on the California coastline, a proud concrete tower on a grassy knoll in Minnesota—these say more about ourselves than do the objects within them. Even though we are often more intrigued by the inaccessible private world of our interiors, our exteriors are an articulate and revealing public presentation of ourselves.

In choosing the colors, materials, and textures that become the exteriors of our homes, we can respond to conditions larger than our personal visions. These choices are inspired by the homes of other times and other places, but they may also derive from the illusions of film, the fantasy in a phrase, the moment in a painting. Our decisions are influenced by what we remember and what we never saw at all.

The colors we use are inherent in the materials we select or they are consciously applied to surfaces that we make. Colors change with age and with weather, with shifts of light and of season and of landscape.

The colors of brick and stone can be formal and austere or they can be familiar and gracious. Adobe and ice are carved from beneath our feet to make pueblos and igloos of earth tones and whites. Stainless steel panels wrap Silverstream trailers, and white porcelain forms the building blocks for abstract "machines for living." Tents, like synthetic cocoons, surround and protect in unnatural hues. Rough-hewn logs are piled and sealed with mud to make log cabins in the natural tones of the materials used. Grayed shingles face the Northeast Coast. Houseboats in Seattle are painted plywood boxes. In towns from Nantucket to Mendocino, colors used in concert transcend their individual strengths.

Yet these possibilities in themselves hold no value. It is in the hand of the maker that color takes on meaning. The pictures and words of this book show how, like a painter at a canvas, we make choices of scale and proportion, atmosphere and mood, in the making of our homes. And how, like a playwright, we can elicit feelings of hope and joy, melancholy and nostalgia.

With color, we can be serious or we can be absurd. We can offer the unsettling or the serene. We hold the power to surprise and delight.

NATE MCBRIDE, *June 1993*

# TAKE A HOUSE AND CHANGE ITS COLOR

Color is the single most effective way to alter the personality of a building. It can make a serious facade flirtatious, an undistinguished one memorable. The color of a house can also affect the landscape, complementing the arbor of red roses or lessening the green-black bulk of an ancient cedar. Of course, color can also be disastrous. How many innocent people have pictured a delicate peach exterior, only to be mortified to see a shade closer to terra-cotta once the paint has dried? Such shocks are understandable because color selection is never easy. Paint samples are not truly helpful: a paint chip is tiny, a house is large, and the mental leap from one to the other is immense.

Modern technology has several solutions. When video computer imaging becomes more accessible, a home owner will be able to go to a video monitor station, select from its menu a facade similar to that of his or her house, and wait a moment while the magic microchips show what the homestead will look like sheathed in brick, paint, ceramic tiles, or any number of textures. Another button produces a variety of colors for the facade as well as for the trims. When finished, vibrant color printouts enable owners to realize the perfect color for the house of their dreams. It will not be long before paint distributors—like professional image consultants—will also rely on computers to simplify the choice of colors.

Already the ColorVision system developed by Interlux, for example, uses computers to help boat owners choose a unique color combination for their sailboats. A digitized photo image of the

boat appears on an Amiga video monitor, and by manipulating a track ball and cursor, one thousand colors can be "brushed" onto the image at will. Kodak and Polaroid have also patented similar products that allow the average home photographer to alter the color of a shirt or add golden highlights to a child's blond hair. Though the need for this intriguing—and still expensive—science remains to some a matter of debate, people interested in playing with the colors of their homes have a low-tech alternative at their fingertips.

Few of us are artists, but almost everyone can draw simple squares and rectangles. The easiest way to make a drawing is to photograph the house from across the street, if possible, taking care to choose a camera angle that is as nearly head on as possible and a time of day when the entire facade is completely in light or shade. Have the photograph printed in a comfortable working size, probably 8 × 10 inches. Then lay a sheet of tracing paper over the photograph and draw the outlines of the house and its doors, windows, and trim. If the house has a tree or plantings, trace the outlines of those as well, but keep the drawing simple. (If you are comfortable sketching with a pencil and ruler, you can draw the front of your house without the photograph.) Once you have the outline in pencil, draw over the lines in ink. Next, make photocopies—as many as you like—on 8½ × 11-inch paper. These copies will form a workbook for planning your personal color scheme. Using ideas from this book, or from magazines and neighbors' houses, color the walls, details, and trim of the house with crayons, felt-tip pens, watercolors, or a combination of several techniques. Make at least two or three color schemes before making a final decision. For each color scheme, be sure to color all natural objects, such as grass, trees, foundation plantings, and rocks.

The result of this rudimentary sketch may not be perfect, but it will allow you to feel the effects that different color combinations bring, and to compare them to other color schemes, without the expense of painters, paints, and stains. Once you have settled on a color and have found a paint chip to match, experiment again on several walls of your house to see if you are on the right track. Always remember that the same color looks different if it's matte or glossy or if it's a stain. Live with it awhile to see if you like it, then throw caution to the winds and paint the house. The pleasure of color will be ample reward for your efforts.

# NOTES

2 " Savage nations, uneducated people": Johann Wolfgang von Goethe, *Goethe's Theory of Colors*, p. 55.

2 " 'I wanted to paint' ": quoted by Peter de Francia, *Fernand Léger*, p. 133.

2 "A fundamental truth": Le Corbusier quoted by Miller et al., "Color in Architecture," *AIA Journal*, p. 41.

## INTRODUCTION

8 "True, whitewashing was the earliest form": A. Lawrence Kocher, "Color in Early American Architecture," p. 278.

9 "The painter Wassily Kandinsky": Wassily Kandinsky, *Concerning the Spiritual in Art*, pp. 38–40.

9 "Goethe thought he could": Karl Gerstner, *The Forms of Color*, p. 163.

9 "And Helen Keller once": Leatrice Eiseman, *Alive with Color*, p. 202.

9 "Blue meant mercy": Eiseman, p. 179.

9 "On a sweltering day": Eiseman, p. 179.

9 "And mosquitoes bite": Eiseman, p. 203.

10 "The charred wood of": Tore Drange et al., *Gamle Trehus*, p. 137.

10 "In his *Natural History*": Ralph Mayer, *The Artist's Handbook of Materials and Techniques*, p. 18.

10 "In the southwestern United States": Mary Mix Foley, *The American House*, p. 43.

10 "In England, pink and red": Tom Porter, *Architectural Color*, p. 37.

10 ". . . by the end of": John Crosby Freeman, "Grand Illusions," p. 67.

10 "any ancient building of ": Ward James, *Colour and Decoration of Architecture*, p. 8.

10 "Herodotus described the city": Porter, *Architectural Color*, p. 16.

12 "Even Notre Dame cathedral": Nory Miller et al., "Color in Architecture," p. 41.

12 "With the Reformation": Porter, *Architectural Color*, p. 18.

12 "Such religious fervor": James Ward, *Colour Decoration of Architecture*, p. 7.

12 "A century or so later": Andrew Sim, "True Colors," *Traditional Homes*, p. 34.

12 "But Counter-Reformation was": Roger Moss, "You Can't Paint 'Em White Anymore," *Historic Preservation*, p. 50.

12 "In the view of critic": Roger Moss and Gail Caskey Winkler, *Victorian Exterior Decoration*, p. 19.

12 ". . . and for John Ruskin": Lauren S. Weingarden, "The Colors of Nature," *Winterthur Portfolio*, p. 244.

12 "Victorian tastemakers ruled": Moss and Winkler, *Victorian Exterior Decoration*, p. 19.

12 ". . . houses should show man": Weingarden, "The Colors of Nature," p. 244.

13 "He introduced a new": Porter, *Architectural Color*, p. 18.

13 "'Nature has enhanced'": Miller et al., "Color in Architecture," *AIA Journal*, p. 58.

## WHITE

15 "Blow trumpet,": Alfred, Lord Tennyson, *The Coming of Arthur*, 481.

## YELLOW

29 "The sun, which sees": Homer, *The Iliad*, Book III, 277.

29 "In imperial China": Johannes Itten, *The Art of Color*, p. 17.

## TAN

41 "Things are seldom": W. S. Gilbert, *H. M. S. Pinafore*, Act II.

## ORANGE

52 "Orange is like": Kandinsky, *Concerning the Spiritual in Art*, p. 41.

## RED

66 "And let's be": William Shakespeare, *The Winter's Tale*, Act IV, Scene iv.

## PINK

78 "The very pink": Oliver Goldsmith, *She Stoops to Conquer*, Act I.

## BROWN

92 "Brown is . . . grave": George Field, *Rudiments of the Painter's Art*, pp. 92–93.

92 "Discussing the building": Vincent Scully, *American Architecture and Urbanism*, p. 84.

## BLUE

105 "Blue color is everlastingly": John Ruskin, *Lectures on Architecture and Painting*.

## GRAY

114 "Dear friend,": Johann Wolfgang von Goethe, *Faust*, Part I, Scene iv.

114 ". . . J. M. W. Turner relied": Faber Birren, *Principles of Color*, pp. 62–63.

## GREEN

128 "My salad days": Shakespeare, *Antony and Cleopatra*, Act I, Scene v.

128 "On a visit to America": Moss et al., "Color in Architecture," *AIA Journal*, p. 97.

## MULTI

142 "He best can paint": Alexander Pope, *Eloisa to Abelard*, 366.

# BIBLIOGRAPHY

Agoston, George A. *Color Theory and Its Application in Art & Design*. New York: Springer-Verlag, 1979. A technical book with many tables and charts.

Aitchison, Prof. "Colored Buildings." *American Architect* 82 (Oct. 17, 1903), pp. 19–20. Lecture originally delivered to the Royal Institute of British Architects. Points out importance of color on exterior of buildings.

————. "An Essay in Color Architecture." *The Architectural Review* 21 (Mar. 1907), pp. 159–173. Glazed building materials as practical and permanent decoration in the dirt and corrosiveness of the urban environment.

Albers, Josef. *Interaction of Color*. New Haven: Yale University Press, 1971. Conceived as a guide and teaching aid for artists, instructors, and students. Mostly about mixing colors together, including experiments with cutout pieces of colored paper.

Banov, Abel. *Book of Successful Painting*. Farmington, Mich.: Structures Publishing Co., 1975. The purpose of this book is to keep the cost and bother of painting to a minimum. It even shows how to balance a ladder properly and how to prepare plywood.

Berenson, Bernard. *Aesthetics and History in the Visual Arts*. New York: Pantheon Books, 1948. Berenson writes that color is of prime importance, exploring its role in jewels, artifacts, textiles, stained glass, statuary, and painting.

Bergheim, Laura A. *Weird Wonderful America*. New York: Macmillan Publishing Co., 1988. The nation's most offbeat and off-the-beaten-path tourist attractions.

Betsky, Aaron. "Desert Bloom." *Architectural Record*, mid-Apr. 1990, pp. 65–69. Stresses architecture's connection with the natural landscape.

Birren, Faber. *Color Perception in Art*. West Chester, Penn.: Schiffer Publishing Ltd., 1986. A summary by a great colorist.

————. *Principles of Color*. New York: Van Nostrand Reinhold, 1969. A good overview of color theory, especially the chapter called "History of Color Circles."

Bliss, Anna Campbell. "Art, Color, Architecture: Their Synergy Explored." *AIA Journal* 71 (Feb. 1982), pp. 48–55. Links art, color, and architecture in the history of modern art.

Candee, Richard M. *Housepaints in Colonial America*. New York: Chromatic Publishing Co., 1967. Sections on the preparation, sale, storage, and application of paint for both interior and exterior use. Detailed but fun to read.

————. "Materials Toward a History of Housepaints." Doctoral dissertation, State University College at Oneonta (New York), 1965. Akin to the above.

Cerwinske, Laura. *Miami: Hot & Cool*. New York: Clarkson N. Potter, 1990. Photographs by Steven Brooke and generally informative.

Chevreul, M. E. *Color*. New York: Time-Life Books, 1971. How color photography works: techniques, examples, and history.

————. *The Principles of Harmony and Contrast of Colors*. New York: Van Nostrand Reinhold, 1967. Based on the first English edition of 1854 as translated from *De la Loi du Contraste Simultané des Couleurs*, 1839. Introduction and notes by Faber Birren. Original, seminal work and the first to stress color in the human experience of vision. Repetitious and possibly overrated.

"Color in Industry—The Anglo-Saxon Is Released From Chromatic Inhibitions. With spectrophoto-electric curves he prepares to outdo the barbarians." *Fortune* I:1, pp. 85–94. Writing in the first edition of *Fortune* magazine more than sixty years ago, the (unknown) author shows that objects—from automobiles to gas pumps to locomotives to bathtubs to skyscrapers are more spectacular in many colors: "Alone among the arts which serve industry, architecture lags behind in the rush to know and use color. When at length it comes into stride, it can make the most spectacular exhibition of all . . . And all our poets will applaud."

Conran, Terence. *The House Book*. New York: Crown Publishers, 1976. Every aspect of decorating a house, inside and out.

Cousens, C. W. "Paint, Architecturally Considered." *American Architect* 122: 2401 (Aug. 30, 1922), pp. 175–176. Paint as used to renovate and increase civic pride.

Cutler, Carl Gordon, and Stephen C. Pepper. *Modern Color*. Cambridge: Harvard University Press, 1923. Mostly color technique for painters and the effects of different colors.

De Francia, Peter. *Fernand Léger*. New Haven: Yale University Press, 1983. Contains good bits about Léger's views on color and architecture.

Delevoy, Robert L. *Léger*. Paris: Editions d'Art Albert Skira, 1962. Chapter on painting and architecture called "The Lure of the Wall."

Devoe (F. W.) and Company. *Exterior Decoration: A Treatise on the Artistic Use of Colors in the Ornamentation on Buildings*. Philadelphia: The Athenaeum of Philadelphia, 1976. Originally published 1885. Good modern introduction with notes on early paint history and Victorian paint use. Useful bibliography as well as plates showing how houses change when painted in different colors.

Drange, Tore, Hans Olaf Aanensen, and Jon Braenne. *Gamle Trehus: Reparasion og Vedlikehold*. Oslo: Universitetsforlaget, 1980. Interesting and extremely useful text on history, construction, and maintenance of Norwegian wooden homes. Includes very long, detailed chapter (pp. 135–180) on color and decoration with historical notes as well as color charts for both exteriors and interiors.

Duttman, Martina, Friedrich Schmuck, and J. Uhl. *Color in Townscape*. San Francisco: W. H. Freeman and Co., 1981. Good chapter on the history of color classification systems.

Duveen, Edward J. *Colour in the Home*. London: George Allen and Co., 1911.

Repetitive, dealing mainly with interiors and which colors look best together.

Eiseman, Leatrice. *Alive with Color*. Washington: Acropolis Books, 1983. How to improve the quality of life through use of color. Some useful background on color symbolism.

Emmerling, Mary Elisor. *American Country*. New York: Clarkson N. Potter, 1980. Life with American antique furniture and accessories.

———. *American Country Classics*. New York: Clarkson N. Potter, 1990. A guide to the way America lives with the style of American Country. Separated into chapters along stylistic lines: Traditional, Romantic, Rustic, Eclectic.

Epstein, Jason, and Elizabeth Barlow. *East Hampton: A History and Guide*. New York: Random House, 1985. History and sightseers' guide, including information on the significance of East Hampton's houses and landscapes.

Farm Buildings Advisory Committee. *Colour Finishes for Farm Buildings*. London: Design Council, 1975. Recommended colors for farm buildings in England. Tables of recommended combinations and paint chips are included.

Field, George. *Rudiments of the Painters' Art*. London: John Weale, 1850. A little vague and philosophical but has useful lists of pigments and some practical information.

Filler, Martin. "Le Corbusier's True Colors." *House & Garden*, May 1987, pp. 175–226. The disagreement on Villa Savoye's (at Poissy, near Paris) exact colors.

Fogden, Michael and Patricia. *Animals and Their Colors*. New York: Crown Publishers, 1974. How animals use colors in terms of socializing, signaling, and interacting.

Foley, Mary Mix. *The American House*. New York: Harper & Row, 1980. The development of American domestic architecture, tracing the progression of native, folk, and formal traditions. Illustrated with drawings.

Freeman, John Crosby. "Grand Illusions: Victorian House Painting Then and Now" (parts 1 and 2). *Victorian Homes*, summer 1987/fall 1987. Historical look at the use of color on Victorian homes from 1840 to the present.

Gagne, Cole. "Glossary of Historic Paints." *Old House Journal*, May 1986, pp. 178–179. Good, concise listing of paints and pigments used in America from the eighteenth to mid-nineteenth centuries.

Garnsey, Julian Ellsworth. "Space, Light and Color." *Journal of the A.I.A.* 13 (June 1920), pp. 251–256. An article showing how architects must always be aware of color.

Gass, William. *On Being Blue: A Philosophical Inquiry*. Boston: David R. Godine, 1975. An exploration of the color blue, usually as an erotic hue.

Gatz, Konrad, and Gerhard Achterberg. *Colour and Architecture*. New York: Architectural Book Publishing Co., 1967. Originally published in Germany, with much technical information.

Gebhard, David, and Robert Winter. *Architecture in Los Angeles: A Compleat Guide*. Salt Lake City: Peregrine Smith Books,

1985. Guide to the manmade structures, gardens, parks, and other features that make up Los Angeles County.

Geeson, Alfred G. *The Practical Painter and Decorator*. London: Virtue and Co., n.d. Good, charming, and informative on techniques, processes, materials, ornament, history, and even paperhanging and estimating.

Gerstner, Karl. *The Forms of Color*. Cambridge, Mass.: The MIT Press, 1986. The relationship between form and color. Includes discussion of Kandinsky and his painterly geometry.

Goethe, Johann Wolfgang von. *Goethe's Theory of Colors*. London: John Murray, 1840. Goethe's research into the nature of color, including details of his experiments and his spiritual interpretations of the results.

Golden, Frederic. *Quasars, Pulsars, and Black Holes*. New York: Charles Scribner's Sons, 1976. Astronomy, including the meanings of different colors of light and stars.

"Great News About Architecture in Color." *House and Garden*. Sept. 1975, pp. 94–95. Thirteen examples from leading architects who are bringing color into their work.

Grow, Lawrence. *The Third Old House Catalogue*. New York: Macmillan Publishing Co., 1982. Where-to-get-it/how-to-use-it resource for restoring and decorating the period house.

———, and Dina Von Zweck. *American Victorian*. New York: Harper & Row, 1984. Style and source book, mostly about the period's interior design.

Hardy, Alexander C., ed. *Colour in Architecture*. London: Leonard Hill, 1967. Good background, stressing importance of thoroughly understanding color before trying to make it contribute to architecture.

Hubbard, R. H. "In Praise of White Paint." *Royal Architectural Institute of Canada Journal* 33 (Apr. 1955), pp. 118–123. Somewhat biased review of the merits of white paint. Author is on a crusade to "improve . . . our environment" by "convert[ing] others to the cult of white."

Hunter College Art Gallery. *Color Documents: A Presentational Theory*. New York: Hunter College Art Gallery, 1985. A bibliography, accompanying an exhibition listing treatises on color from about the 1750s to the 1960s.

*Identification of Colors for Building*. Washington, D.C.: Building Research Institute, 1962. Compilation of articles and lectures from various sources in the field of color. Concentrates on how to standardize colors and how to match them correctly on the exteriors of buildings.

Isham, Norman M., and Alfred F. Brown. *Early Connecticut Houses: An Historical and Architectural Study*. Providence, R.I.: The Preston and Rounas Co., 1900. Traces the development of planning and the changes of building methods in the seventeenth and eighteenth centuries.

Itten, Johannes. *The Art of Color*. New York: Van Nostrand Reinhold, 1961. Compares the color perspective of the physicist, chemist, physiologist, and artist. Looks at historical use of color by artists from Egyptian times through the Expressionists.

Jenson and Nicholson. *Paint and Its Part in Architecture*. London, 1930. Summary of colors and pigments.

Kandinsky, Wassily. *Concerning the Spiritual in Art*. New York: Dover Publications, 1977. Originally published as *Uber das Geistige in der Kunst*, 1911. Discusses the new principles on which modern art developed. Section called "The Psychological Working of Color" reflects Kandinsky's quest for communication based on color perception and sensation.

Knox, Gerald M., ed. *Living the Country Life*. Des Moines: Meredith Corporation, 1985. A Better Homes and Gardens Book. The "country" look, from both inside and outside the house.

Kocher, A. Lawrence. "Color in Early American Architecture." *Architectural Record* 64 (Oct. 1928), pp. 279–290. Origin and development of early American house painting, both interiors and exteriors. Lists early sources and formulas for mixing paints.

Landau, Robert. *Outrageous L.A.* San Francisco: Chronicle Books, 1984. An effort to pin down the spirit of Los Angeles.

———, Brent K. Smith, and Jennifer Place. *Color in Interior Design and Architecture*. New York: Van Nostrand Reinhold, 1989. Basic approach to color as a design tool. Shows how color can alter the perception of space.

Lasdun, Susan. *Victorians at Home*. New York: The Viking Press, 1981. Chronicle of English homes, 1819–1901.

Laurence, F. S. *Color in Architecture*. New York: National Terra Cotta Society, 1922. How to use polychromy—applied ornament, terra-cotta, or glazed tile—appropriately. Good insights into the fundamental nature of color on buildings.

Laurie, A. P. *The Materials of the Painter's Craft*. Philadelphia: J. P. Lippincott Co., 1911. History of techniques and preparation of paints in Egyptian and Classical eras.

Léger, Fernand. "New York," *Fonctions de la Peinture*. (Originally published in *Cahiers d'Art*, nos. 9–10, 1931 as quoted by Peter de Francia, *Fernand Léger*.)

Martin, James, and Jill Pilaroscia. "Thoughts on Exterior Painting." *Old House Journal* (May 1986), pp. 166–170. How to choose house colors.

Mayer, Ralph. *The Artist's Handbook of Materials and Techniques*. New York: The Viking Press, 1957. Too technical for most needs but a good summary of pigments by color category.

McAlester, Virginia and Lee. *A Field Guide to American Houses*. New York: Alfred A. Knopf, 1984. A guide to identifying houses in typical American neighborhoods. Classifies houses into categories of Folk, Colonial, Romantic, Victorian, Eclectic, or Since 1940 and then divides them by style.

Miller, Kevin H. *Paint Color Research and Restoration of Historic Paint*. The Association for Preservation Technology, 1977. Scientific case studies in paint restoration, preservation, and research. Outstanding bibliography.

Miller, Nory, et al. "Color in Architecture." *AIA Journal* 67:12 (special issue, Oct. 1978). Examples of ways in which architects approach color.

Moss, Roger. *Century of Color*. Watkins Glen, N.Y.: American Life Foundation, 1981. Sherwin-Williams house-painting guide for the Victorian era. Many illustrations of one house painted in several different color combinations.

———. "You Can't Paint 'Em White Anymore." *Historic Preservation* 34 (Jan./Feb. 1982), pp. 50–53. Brief, good look at the history of houses painted white in the United States. Contains a summary as well as a rationalization for white. Discusses the mistaken assumption that Victorian houses were always painted white.

———, and Gail Caskey Winkler. *Victorian Exterior Decoration*. New York: Henry Holt and Co., 1987. How to paint your nineteenth-century American house historically.

Munsell, A. H. *A Color Notation*. Boston: George H. Ellis Co., 1913. How to specify colors with three dimensions: hue, value, and chroma. Concentrates on teaching color concepts to young children.

Newton, Roger Hale. "On the Tradition of Polychromy and Paint of the American Dwelling from Colonial to Present Times." *American Society of Architectural Historians Journal* 3 (July 1943), pp. 21–25, 43. Misconceptions about this country's perceived colonial passion for white.

Patton, Phil. "In Seaside, Florida, the Forward Thing Is to Look Backward." *Smithsonian*, Jan. 1991, pp. 82–93. History and description of the planned community of Seaside, Florida.

Podolsky, Edward, M.D. *The Doctor Prescribes Colors*. New York: National Library Press, 1938. Influence of colors on health and personality.

Pomada, Elizabeth, and Michael Larsen. *Daughters of Painted Ladies: America's Resplendent Victorians*. New York: E. P. Dutton, 1987. The story of "Painted Ladies" as owned by baby boomers.

———. *Painted Ladies*. New York: E. P. Dutton, 1978. Color photographs of painted Victorian houses of San Francisco. Predictable, although introduction has good information.

Poore, Patricia, and Clem Labine. *The Old-House Journal New Compendium*. Garden City, N.Y.: Dolphin Books, 1983. Excellent reference source for old houses. Simple history of paints on American houses plus drawings of various architectural styles with keys indicating suitable colors.

Porter, Tom. *Architectural Color*. New York/London: Watson-Guptill Publications, 1982. Originally published by the Architectural Press Ltd., London, in 1982. Complete and thoughtful work on the relationship between architecture and color.

Reynolds, Hezekiah. *Directions for House and Ship Painting*. Worcester, Mass.: American Antiquarian Society, 1978. Originally printed in 1812, the earliest known American publication compiled by a New England craftsman and not based on English sources.

Ruskin, John. *Seven Lamps of Architecture*. Boston: Dana Estes, n.d. A Victorian view of architecture. Ruskin believed that color is independent of form.

Sanford, John Ithiel. *Sanford's Manual of Color*. New York: Hugh Kelly and Co., 1910. Overview of color from an old-fashioned and slightly simplistic viewpoint.

Schuler, Stanley. *Old New England Homes*. Exton, Penn.: Schiffer Publishing, 1984. History of housing in New England, organized by style.

Scully, Vincent. *American Architecture and Urbanism*. New York: Praeger, 1969. Third printing 1973. Essential narrative to the understanding of urban America. Wonderful writing.

Shay, James. *New Architecture San Francisco*. San Francisco: Chronicle Books, 1989. Photographs by Christopher Irion, with an update on San Francisco's architecture.

Sherwin-Williams Company. "Sherwin-Williams History." 1989. Unpublished leaflet issued by the company on the history of their business and the paint industry.

Sim, Andrew. "True Colors." *Traditional Homes*, Jan./Feb./Mar. 1989. Three-part article on the changing use of color illustrated by the Middle Ages, the Georgian period, and the Victorian age. Stresses English use of color.

Solon, Leon V. *Polychromy: Architectural and Structural Theory and Practice*. New York: The Architectural Record, 1924. Highly intellectual work emphasizing the nature of Greek polychromy.

Southern Accents Press. *Historic Houses of the South*. New York, 1984. Overview of the South's architectural history.

Stoddard, Brooke C. "Picking the Right Paint Color." *Historic Preservation* 39:16 (Sept./Oct. 1987). Historic colors as well as application methods, historic districts, and architectural review boards. Good summary of exterior color schemes for principal architectural styles of the eighteenth and nineteenth centuries.

Swirnoff, Lois. *Dimensional Color*. Boston: Birkhauser, 1988. Chapter on color called "Architecture and the Significance of the Surface." Most examples cited are not American.

Tufte, Edward R. *Envisioning Information*. Cheshire, Conn.: Graphics Press, 1990. How to communicate quantitative information through the combined use of color, words, pictures, and numbers.

Van Zanten, David. *The Architectural Polychromy of the 1830s*. New York: Garland Publishing, Inc., 1977. Originally doctoral dissertation, Harvard, 1970. Uses the architectural polychromy of the 1830s to analyze the relationship between color and geometric form.

"Vivid Color." *Architectural Forum* 103 (Nov. 1955), pp. 124–128. Briefly mentions advances in postwar chemistry—anodizing and enameling processes, brick, aluminum, steel—which have added many colors to the architect's palette.

Ward, James. *Colour Decoration of Architecture*. London: Chapman and Hall, 1913. Some notes on ancient traditions; otherwise mostly about the history of color decoration in Europe.

Weingarden, Lauren S. "The Colors of Nature: Louis Sullivan's Architectural Polychromy . . ." *Winterthur Portfolio* 20 (winter 1985), pp. 243–260. Sullivan's use of color as metaphor. Overview of the prevailing intellectual climate.

Weismantel, Guy E. *Paint Handbook*. New York: McGraw-Hill, 1981. Color from a chemical engineering standpoint and quite technical. Topics include paint fundamentals, surface preparation and coatings, application techniques, economics.

Wilkinson, Sir J. Gardner. *On Color*. London: John Murray, 1858. The author's attempt to make "England rival, and if possible excel, other countries in all the various branches of aesthetic art."

Wolfe, Tom. *From Bauhaus to Our House*. New York: Farrar, Straus & Giroux, 1981. Wolfe's criticism of twentieth-century American architecture, which he dislikes because it's too bare, spare, impersonal, and highly abstract. A thin and overwritten book.

# ACKNOWLEDGMENTS

In 1987 my husband and I finished rebuilding a small house in Stonington, Connecticut, with the help of architect Nate McBride. During this period, Nate also became my son-in-law, a complex but happy evolution. His wife, Kari McCabe, an interior designer, showed us five exterior color schemes that might be suitable for a Colonial house that faces a village on one side, and the sea on the other.

Now, of course, it seems obvious that our house *had* to be blue with white trim and a tangerine-colored door, but at the time, it was a difficult set of decisions. Shortly thereafter, the house appeared on the cover of *Metropolitan Home,* with a spread inside. And within two weeks, Gael Towey—who was then the art director of Clarkson N. Potter—called to say that the president of Crown Publishers had seen the article and asked what she thought of a book about the exteriors of houses.

*Exteriors* is the result of this fortuitous series of events. Originally organized by materials, the book took shape when my friend Peter Jones, who himself is involved in photography and design, simply said why not use color as the organizing element?

He was right, of course, and from there, Lauren Shakely, my wise and witty editor, carried it through with the help of yet another art director, Howard Klein. They were the ones who helped me produce what I hope are the seamless images of *Exteriors*.

Suzanne Goldstein, my photography agent from Photo-Researchers, provided invaluable help in rounding up images and photographers and Alec McCabe helped sort out the early notes. With the assistance of Nina Anson Szarkowski, who put more than five hundred houses, owners, architects, and photographers on a data base, I was able to assemble and shape *Exteriors*. Mitchell Owens ably helped with the captions.

The photographers are an amazing lot —talented and generous. My grateful thanks to Andrew Bordwin, Steven Brooke, Langdon Clay, Geoffrey Clifford, Jacques Dirand, Mick Hales, John M. Hall, Timothy Hursley, Christopher Irion, David Katzenstein, Christopher Little, Norman McGrath, Michael Moran, Michael Mundy, David Phelps, Timothy Street-Porter, Paul Warchol, Susan Wood, and to everyone who contributed from Comstock, Esto, FPG, Image Bank, and Stock Photo. Three photography managers deserve special thanks: Lance Fischbein, Betsy Little, and Erica Stoller.

Louis Gropp of *House Beautiful*, Nancy Novogrod and Carolyn Sollis of *HG*, and Steven Wagner of *Metropolitan Home* continually assisted. Architects Thomas Beebe in Chicago, Joan Goody in Boston, Brian Murphy in Los Angeles, and Carlos Brillembourg, Robert Gatje, and Bartholomew Voorsanger in New York suggested further sources for *Exteriors*. André Emmerich led me to David Hockney, Vincent Scully graciously looked at the photographs, and James Merrill optimistically said that if I put my mind to it, I too could write!

Judi and Gordon Davidon lined up architects and photographers in Los Angeles. And in New York, painter Cornelia Foss and publisher Geraldine Stutz helped me edit by contributing their brilliant vision. Curator Catherine Hoover Voorsanger helped and photographer Rollei McKenna lent me her studio. Home owners were hospitable, especially Pam Lord, Robert Dash, Betsy Wade, James Boylan, and Maria McVitty. Antiquarian Marguerite Riordan took me to Peter Arkel, whose brilliant gray door stands surrounded by glossy tomato-red paint, and Molly McCabe was always a good critic.

My thanks also to my excellent agents, Kristine Dahl and Robert Tabian of International Creative Management. They always returned my phone calls and were unusually helpful whenever the going was rough. And to Joan Denman, Andrea Connolly, Renato Stanisic, and all others at Clarkson Potter.

Final thanks to the Willy Loman of urban America, my husband, Oz Elliott, who with grace and humor can manage hundreds of thousands of people as well as he does a wife.

# INDEX

Adobe, 13, 53, 58, 59, 92, 97, 132, 157
Albert, Prince, 90
Almond green, 136
Aluminum, 111, 114, 118, 149
Aquamarine, 26, 85, 139, 140, 149
Arsenic green, 10
Art Deco, 82
Asphalt, 24
Awnings, striped, 22, 34, 39, 109, 120
Azure, 142

Balcony, 46, 72
Barn, 21, 32, 76, 110
Barrágan, Luis, 13, 61
Beige, 41, 49
Black, 8–10, 13, 18, 37, 39, 86, 114, 120
Blond, 53
Blue, 7–13, 22, 39, 62, 65, 92, 105–113, 114, 127, 137, 142, 149, 150, 152
Boulders, 50
Brick, 49, 62, 72, 73, 91, 100, 110, 128, 134, 135, 157, 159
Bronze, 138
Brown, 9, 71, 86, 92–104, 114, 126, 148, 152
Brownstone, 92, 100, 139
Burgundy, 77
Buttermilk, 24
Butter yellow, 36

Carmine red, 10
Cedar, 44
Cement, 114
Charcoal, 10
Chocolate, 65, 86
Chrome green, 10
Chrome yellow, 10
Cinderblock, 118
Cinnamon, 103
Clapboard, 15, 32–34, 36, 45, 56, 89, 103, 112, 134, 152
Colonial style, 7, 8, 13, 50, 64, 78, 85, 92
Colors, 8–13, 157, 159. *See also specific colors*
Columns, 15, 26, 39, 71, 146
Concrete, 24, 46, 62, 157
Copper, 125
Cornflower blue, 7
Corrugated metal, 97, 124, 157
Cream, 24, 32, 41, 44, 45, 46, 71, 150, 152

Deck, 50
Door, 7, 37, 39, 77, 86, 98, 109, 127, 132, 137, 146, 152
Dutch pink, 8

Eames, Ray and Charles, 148
Emerald green, 136
English red, 9

Fallingwater, 47
Farmhouse, 21, 32, 66, 97, 103
Fence, 85, 114, 118
Fire escape, 64, 76
Floor, 39, 71, 149, 150
French blue, 8

Gate, 71
Gingerbread, 71, 126, 150
Glass, 32, 149
Gold, 10, 71
Gothic Revival, 7, 71, 86, 126
Graffiti, 61
Granite, 138
Graves, Michael, 13
Gray, 7–8, 26, 39, 45, 62, 85, 90, 97, 103, 114–127, 152, 157
Greek Revival, 7, 15, 27, 61, 98
Green, 7, 8, 10, 21, 35, 37, 61, 62, 66, 92, 114, 125, 128–141, 142, 152
Greene, Charles S. and Henry M., 98

Hardware, 37, 127
Hardy, Hugh, 13
Honey, 24, 50
Hunt, Richard Morris, 49

Indian red, 8
Indigo, 8
Iron, 61, 65, 77
Iron oxide, 9
Italian Renaissance, 120
Ivory, 10, 25

Jade green, 128
Jones, Inigo, 12

Kelly green, 18
King's yellow, 8

Lavender, 112
Le Corbusier, 13
Lemon yellow, 35
Lime, 112, 128
Limestone, 45, 85, 120
Logs, 53, 103, 118, 157

Magenta, 142
Marble, 13, 15, 41, 49
Marble House, 49
Materials, 24, 56, 72, 85, 92, 157. *See also specific materials*
McKim, Mead, and White, 15
Mediterranean style, 29, 86
Metal, 56, 71, 118
Metallic paints, 114
Ming yellow, 146
Modern style, 13, 22
Molding, 37
Mondrian, Piet, 13, 149
Multi-colored, 142–155
Mustard yellow, 29, 36, 39

Neoclassical style, 12, 15
Notre Dame cathedral, 12

Ocher, 9, 10, 29
Orange, 9–10, 13, 53–65, 114, 132, 142, 152

Palladio, 12, 46
Pastels, 71, 89
Peach, 53, 65
Peacock blue, 136
Pearl, 8
Pink, 8, 10, 78–91, 128, 149
Plywood, 24
Porcelain, 157
Porch, 39, 71, 90, 109, 150
Prussian blue, 10
Pumpkin, 134
Purple, 105, 112, 142

Raspberry, 89, 90
Red, 7–13, 21–23, 34, 39, 41, 44, 53, 59, 61, 66–77, 89, 92, 127, 128, 150, 152
Roof, 18, 21, 44, 64, 65, 72, 85, 86, 90, 110, 146, 152
Rose, 65, 86

Royal blue, 111
Ruskin, John, 12
Rust, 151

Saint-Gaudens, Augustus, 71
Salmon, 64, 150
Sandstone, 50, 100
Scarlet, 132, 146
Scully, Vincent, 100
Sea foam green, 138
Sheet metal, 151
Shingles, 7, 24, 44, 56, 98, 126, 132, 157
Shutters, 2, 22, 26, 39, 61, 62, 64, 72, 78, 85, 103, 109, 112, 120, 128, 134
Shutze, Philip Trammell, 46
Siding, 15, 24, 44, 50, 56, 111
Sienna, 9, 59, 62, 98
Silo, 103
Silver, 10, 58, 97
Slate, 64
Snow, 21, 66, 138
Stairway, 61, 125, 140

Steel, 32, 103, 114, 125, 146, 157
Steps, 45, 85, 140
Stone, 41, 44, 45, 49, 91, 92, 114, 152, 157
Stucco, 18, 26, 36, 39, 41, 44, 56, 71, 88, 109, 114, 118, 120, 125, 126, 146, 149

Tan, 7, 13, 41–51, 56, 109, 126
Tangerine, 7
Tepee, 22
Tiles, 29, 41, 88, 114, 146, 152, 159
Tin, pressed, 85
Trim, 7, 8, 15, 18, 24, 34, 35, 62, 76, 86, 88, 91, 127
Turner, J. M.W., 114
Turquoise, 26, 138, 150
Tuscan style, 88

Ultramarine, 8, 10, 132
Umber, 8, 10

Van der Rohe, Mies, 13
Vaux, Calvert, 12

Venturi, Robert, 13
Veranda, 24
Victorian style, 7, 8, 13, 78, 86, 88, 91, 92
Vines, 64, 73, 135
Violet, 65, 105

Walkway, 39
Walls, 21, 36, 41, 44, 53, 56, 57, 61, 64, 65, 66, 71, 72, 86, 88, 91, 97, 112, 127, 132, 135, 137, 146, 152
Water, 97
White, 7–14, 15–27, 32–34, 44, 49, 61, 62, 66, 71, 76, 92, 97, 100, 103, 109, 114, 125, 126, 139, 146, 157
Windows, 18, 21, 32, 39, 53, 61, 72, 73, 85, 88, 98, 103, 109, 112, 134, 135, 146, 152
Wood, 26, 49, 50, 71, 76, 98, 114, 118, 124, 149
Wright, Frank Lloyd, 47
Wrought iron, 86

Yellow, 7–13, 29–39, 53, 58, 65, 71, 120, 132, 142, 146, 152

# CREDITS